# The Psychology of
# Persuasion
## *Influence Others with Ease*

# Table of Contents

# Chapter 1. Introduction

Are you ready to navigate the fascinating labyrinth of the human mind? Welcome to our Special Report on "The Psychology of Persuasion: Influence Others with Ease." This riveting exploration isn't just an academic romp, oh no, it's a practical guide to tapping into the incredible power of persuasion we all possess! Often overlooked, our ability to persuade can be a transformative tool when understood and used effectively. Whether you're pitching a breakthrough idea, influencing decisions, or just encouraging your kids to eat their vegetables, this special report boasts a cornucopia of strategies backed by psychological insights, helping you influence others effortlessly. Peek under the bonnet of human behavior and turbocharge your persuasive power - all with a sense of fun, engagement, and ethical sense of influence. Unleash the convincing communicator within you today by delving into this enthralling Special Report!

# Chapter 2. The Fundamentals: Understanding Persuasion

Persuasion draws its roots from the depths of human psychology. Boiling it down to its most basic definition, persuasion is the skill of changing or reinforcing attitudes, beliefs, values, or behaviors. But it's far more than just a simple verbal trick. It's an art form rooted in understanding and empathy, grounded in knowing your audience and speaking to them directly.

## 2.1. The Birth of Persuasion

It's important to consider where persuasion originates in the grand scope of our development as a species. Persuasion wasn't something we humans just stumbled upon recently — it has been a crucial part of our evolution and survival. Early humans used persuasion to work together, to convince others to follow certain paths or undertake certain tasks for the betterment of the group. The ability to persuade was Darwinian in nature, contributing to survival and the propagation of the species.

In short, persuasion has been a valuable adaptive trait, engrained into the very fabric of our social interactions. As a result, its study and application have been a critical endeavor throughout history.

## 2.2. Psychological Aspects of Persuasion

Cognitive psychologist Robert Cialdini once proposed that when people are uncertain, they look to others for guidance. They're seeking validation, a path that others approve of and follow. This is known as social proof, and it's one of the fundamental psychological aspects of persuasion.

Social proof is all around us, from online reviews and testimonials to follower counts on social media. It is a powerful persuasion tool because it leverages our inherent social nature as humans. We seek acceptance and approval from our peers, and we tend to do what we see others doing.

Beyond social proof, scarcity also plays a significant role in the psychology of persuasion. Scarcity creates the perception of value. Think of the limited-time offers and the exclusive deals that create a sense of urgency to buy. When resources are scarce, they appear more attractive, and we are more likely to engage or purchase.

Similarly, authority figures also tend to be persuasive. We are more likely to be influenced or persuaded by figures of authority since we perceive them as more knowledgeable or credible. Using symbols of authority, such as titles and uniforms, can significantly increase the persuasiveness of a message or person.

# 2.3. The Art of Persuasion

Persuasion is an art form, and like all art forms, it has techniques, theories, and methods. Among these are the ethos, pathos, and logos approach.

**Ethos,** or ethical persuasion, speaks to your character and credibility. It relies on your reputation or standing in a group or society. When your audience trusts you, they are more likely to be persuaded by your words or actions.

**Pathos,** or emotional persuasion, targets your audience's emotions. It requires you to understand their feelings, fears, and desires. Stories, anecdotes, and powerful imagery are frequently used tools in pathos persuasion.

**Logos,** or logical persuasion, appeals to your audience's intellect. It's about providing clear, logical arguments backed by evidence. Facts, statistics, and expert opinions are often employed in logos persuasion.

# 2.4. Behavior and Persuasion

Perception, cognition, and behavior are interwoven aspects of the human psyche. Our perception influences how we process information (cognition), affecting our actions (behavior).

Many behavioral research studies have found a dynamic relationship between attitudes and behavior. Indeed, our attitudes often drive our behaviors, but it is equally noteworthy that our actions can shape our attitudes. This concept is known as cognitive dissonance, coined by social psychologist Leon Festinger.

According to cognitive dissonance theory, we strive for internal consistency. When we experience inconsistency (dissonance), it results in discomfort, driving us to adjust our attitudes and beliefs to match our behavior.

Persuasion techniques often leverage this knowledge, inducing a behavior to subsequently adjust a person's attitude. This method is sometimes referred to as the "foot-in-the-door" technique, where a smaller initial request is used to increase compliance for a larger request later.

# 2.5. The Ethics of Persuasion

While persuasion is a powerful tool, it is essential to discuss its ethical aspect. Persuasion is not about manipulation or deceit. Instead, it's about understanding, empathy, and communication.

The power of persuasion must be used responsibly and ethically. This means respecting others' autonomy, considering their best interests, and always striving for honesty and transparency.

The psychological underpinnings of persuasion aren't just instruments for selfish gain; they are tools for meaningful interaction, mutual understanding, and progress.

# 2.6. Closing the Loop: The Journey of Persuasion

Understanding persuasion doesn't end with identifying strategies and techniques. It's about understanding human nature, needs, motivations, and emotions.

This guide is a stepping stone towards that comprehension. Mastering persuasion involves cultivating sensitivity towards others, critical thinking, and clear communication skills. It's a journey that can lead to better relationships, successful negotiations, and ultimately, a more empathetic approach towards our interactions with others.

By harnessing the power of persuasion, we can not only influence but also foster understanding, shape shared reality, and help cultivate positive, constructive behaviors. This, in essence, is what makes the study of persuasion a necessary and exciting journey.

# Chapter 3. Realizing Your Innate Power: Unleashing the Persuader within You

In conversation, individuals often bemoan missed opportunities or lament a lack of power in their personal and professional lives. Strangely enough, these same individuals overlook a potent, innate capability innate to all of us - the power of persuasion. Understanding this overlooked tool can open doors, be transformative, and leave an indelible impact. But where do we start in decoding the nuances of this all-pervading influence?

# Chapter 4. Understanding the Power Within

Imagine the persuasion as a seed planted within us. Like the seed's potential to grow into a towering oak, the potential to persuade lies within us all. The only difference? The seed doesn't have the option to ignore its potential - we, on the other hand, often do.

To harness this innate power, the first step is acknowledgment - understanding that you have an intrinsic, powerful capacity to influence others. Acknowledging this potential can imbue confidence, banishing the ephemeral shadows of self-doubt. Studies show that once we believe in our abilities, we are more likely to engage, take risks, and manifest our potential.

# Chapter 5. Unleashing the Power

To effectively wield this power, we must first understand its basis. What are the key facets of persuasive communication? They boil down to three: ethos (credibility), pathos (emotional connection), and logos (logical argument).

## 5.1. Ethos: Cultivating Credibility

Ethos underscores the importance of being perceived as credible and trustworthy. This impression is often instilled prior to your argument. Here's why:

*Trust*: Individuals tend to believe someone they trust. Building trust is the first tenet in engaging your audience.

*Expertise*: Demonstrating expertise in the specifics empowers your words, as the audience tends to believe in the insights of a specialist.

*Similarity*: People are more likely to be persuaded by those who they think are similar to them in some way.

Establishing ethos is an ongoing process, possibly even a pre-emptive step before any direct attempt at persuasion.

# 5.2. Pathos: Emotion Connect

Pathos pertains to connecting with the audience on an emotional level. This connection often drives decision-making, overriding even logical thought.

*Storytelling*: This is a powerful way to attach emotion to an idea. A well-spun story can move an audience, establishing a stronger connect.

*Mutual Experiences*: Shared experiences create a bond. Framing your arguments within the context of shared experiences enhances pathos.

Remember, pathos can be a double-edged sword - it's important to ethically handle this aspect.

# 5.3. Logos: The Logic Link

Logos involves using evidence and logical arguments to persuade. A straight path of reasoning backed by hard facts can be a powerful persuader.

*Evidence*: Authentic, verifiable evidence lends credibility and strength to your persuasion.

*Structured Argument*: A logical, well-structured argument gives clarity to your views, helping the audience grasp your point.

# Chapter 6. Imparting Substance

Just as the rays of light pass through a prism to reveal a spectrum of colors, the simple act of communicating a message should ideally pass through the prism of substance to reveal a spectrum of persuasive charm. Injecting substance into your ethos, pathos, and logos can propel your persuasiveness.

## 6.1. Bias and Perception: A Human Reality

Humans have built-in biases that influence perception. Acknowledging this can help in effective persuasion. Framing, anchoring, and priming are strategies leveraging cognitive biases to enhance your persuasive power.

## 6.2. Mastering the Art of Listening

Persuasion isn't a one-way street. It involves listening, understanding, and addressing the concerns of your audience. Active listening fosters respect, understanding, and trust - three essential components for effective persuasion.

# Chapter 7. Tying it All Together

Enabling the seed of persuasion to bloom requires a concoction of self-belief, understanding of ethos, pathos, and logos, focusing on substance, leveraging biases, and mastering the art of listening. With these tools, we are not just persuading; we are connecting, motivating, and inspiring. Unleashing the persuader within you is an adventure, constantly evolving, and will carry your voice, influence, and passion across the receptivity of human minds.

# Chapter 8. Secrets of Non-Verbal cues: Communicating without Words

In the symphony of communication, words are often just one instrument. They contribute their melodies and nuanced notes, but a richer, more profound language is also at play: the language of non-verbal cues. The fascinating world of body language, facial expressions, and micro-gestures, to name a few, can have immense persuasive power.

Mapping out this complex territory involves looking at different aspects of non-verbal communication that influence our interpretation of messages and how we, consciously or subconsciously, sway others to our point of view. As we dive deep into these layers, we will discuss, analyze, and understand the techniques that can augment our persuasive prowess.

## 8.1. The Power of Posture

Picture this: Two individuals walk into a business meeting. One slouches and avoids eye contact, while the other strides in confidently, standing tall. Whom are you inclined to trust more? The second individual, right? That's the power of posture.

A posture that suggests confidence and openness can unconsciously signal to others that we are credible and trustworthy, instantly bolstering our credibility. Simultaneously, adopting a self-assured posture can also psychologically equip us with feelings of confidence and power, enhancing our persuasiveness.

## 8.2. Navigating the Ocean of Facial Expressions

Faces are like open books, readily revealing our inner emotions. Our joy, sorrow, anger, confusion, and myriad other feelings are all exhibited plainly on our faces. These expressions can play an integral part in how effectively we persuade others. Authentic smiles, for example, can build rapport, fostering a sense of trust and likability.

Being aware of our expressions, including maintaining eye contact, can also allow us to respond aptly to others, showing empathy and understanding. It can also help us decode the non-verbal responses of our audience, enabling us to adapt our approach during the act of persuasion.

## 8.3. Unraveling the Language of Gestures

The significance of gestures in effective communication cannot be overstated. Emphatic gestures can underline our words, reinforcing our points and projecting enthusiasm, which often makes us more persuasive. Conversely, crossed arms or closed off body language can inadvertently signal resistance or discomfort.

By tuning into our gestures and those of others, we gain an additional level of understanding, enabling more effective, persuasive communication. It's about aligning our words and our movements, so they convey the same message and elicit the desired response.

## 8.4. Power-Packed Proxemics: The Rule of Personal Space

How close or far we stand while interacting with others, known as proxemics, is another critical piece of the non-verbal communication puzzle. Manipulating personal spaces can induce psychological responses in the other person, making them more susceptible to our influence.

With proxemics, there is a fine line between making someone comfortable and invading their personal space. Striking the right balance can increase likability and trust, essential factors in persuasion.

## 8.5. The Silent Signals of Haptics

Touch, or haptics, is another non-verbal cue that influences how others perceive us. A good handshake often conveys confidence and creates a positive first impression, aiding the persuasion process. Yet, it's not just about firm handshakes but also about knowing when and how touch can be used appropriately in different cultures and social contexts to augment our persuasive attempts.

## 8.6. Decoding Paralinguistic Cues

Lastly, our tone, pitch, and speed of speaking – our paralinguistic cues – play a fundamental role in how we are perceived. Speaking too fast may come across as rushed or nervous, while speaking too slow can appear disinterested or dull.

By paying attention and adjusting these cues, we can increase our persuasiveness. A simple change of tone can shift a statement from sounding aggressive to assertive or shift a request from demanding to negotiable.

Non-verbal cues are crucial to our communication and persuasive efforts, often carrying more weight than our words. By understanding and mastering the secrets of these cues, we can enhance our ability to influence others, enabling us to communicate more effectively and persuasively.

This investigation into the realm of non-verbal cues reminds us of their importance and their latent potential to imbue our efforts at communication with nuance and impact. The exciting takeaway here is that we have a world of unspoken influence at our fingertips - literally. We need to tune into this universal, yet under the radar, language to make our words and intentions clearer, thereby elevating our persuasive power. Delving into the world of non-verbal cues is not only an interesting exploration of human behavior but also a strategic tool for becoming more effective communicators and influencers.

# Chapter 9. The Psychology of Language: Crafting Powerful Messages

What is summoned by the word "revolution" or "advancement"? Our navigational choices, behaviours, and even feelings are directed by the words we use and hear. This is the profound influence language holds on us.

## 9.1. The Power of the Right Word

Throughout history, political leaders, marketers, and communication experts have harnessed this unique power. They've discovered that tweaking even a single phrase or word within a message can significantly change the reaction of the receiving audience. By examining the impact of effective language use, we unearth the profound connection between the art of persuasion and the science of psychology. Let's delve into the mechanisms that pack persuasive power into words, sentences, and stories, unlocking our potential to craft powerful messages.

We begin with an analysis of an elementary and seemingly innocuous component of language: words.

Words are not merely a combination of random letters; they are packets of meaning, carrying rich evocative potential. A single word can trigger a flurry of emotions, memories, and associations, and these reactions determine the listener's receptivity to your message.

The best communicators know how to wield words skillfully, priming their listeners with subtle cues that shape interpretation and build rapport. For example, by choosing words that have positive associations for your audience, you can create a positive frame that, in turn, enhances their perception of your message.

The effectiveness of this technique lies in the psychological principle of priming, where exposure to a stimulus influences the response to a subsequent stimulus.

# 9.2. Persuasive Language Techniques

So, how do we practically apply these insights to enhance our persuasive prowess? Below are the contours of some impactful persuasive language techniques:

1. Use of Strong Active Verbs: Active verbs inject your message with energy and clarity, making it more dynamic. "The team achieved the target" is more compelling than "The target was achieved by the team".

2. Sensory Language: Descriptions that engage the senses create vivid experiences in the reader's mind and lead to further engagement with your message.

3. Emotional Language: Words that invoke emotion can significantly intensify a message's impact. Advertisers often use emotionally charged words to grab attention and spur action.

4. Linguistic Simplicity: Simplicity trumps complexity. Outsmart your competition with clear, concise, and easy-to-understand language.

5. Repetition: Repetition is a powerful tool that can make your message stick. When used properly, it can enhance memory recall and reinforce your main points.

# 9.3. Framing a Message for Impact

Beyond individual words, the framing of your message plays a pivotal role in its persuasive power. Framing involves mindfully creating an angle or perspective that highlights certain aspects of your message above others.

The science of framing relies heavily on the prospect theory, which suggests that people make decisions based on the potential value of losses and gains. This means we can be influenced to choose one option over another based on how it is framed – whether it is presented as a potential loss or gain.

For example, we are generally more likely to favor messages that emphasize gains or benefits and avoid those involving potential losses or risks. Harnessing this bias in our framing can steer audiences towards certain choices, amplifying our persuasive power.

# Chapter 10. Storytelling: The Ultimate Persuasive Tool

The ultimate embodiment of the power of persuasive language is storytelling. Stories can move us, inspire us, and, above all, persuade us. They enable audiences to experience a situation from a personal perspective, fostering empathy and creating a deep emotional connection.

From a psychological viewpoint, stories are an effective tool for persuasion because they involve a process called transportation. This process pulls us into the narrative world, engaging our emotions, captivating our attention, and facilitating a stronger connection with the message.

Neuroscience research uncovered a phenomenon called neural coupling, which shows that a listener's brain patterns during a story can mirror those of the storyteller, creating a profound empathic connection. So, using storytelling in our messages fosters this connection, making our message more influential.

In conclusion, by understanding the psychology of language, we can master our ability to craft powerful messages that resonate and persuade. The careful use of words, effective framing, and the power of stories is a potent combination that can enhance our influence and amplify our ability to lead, whether in business, community, or personal pursuits.

The path to becoming a more influential communicator is a journey of understanding and applying the psychological principles embedded within our language. By mastering these skills, you'll unlock your true potential to touch hearts, change minds, and make a difference!

# Chapter 11. Strategies of Influence: The Art of Ethical Manipulation

Emphasizing the word "ethical" as our operative term, we anchor our discussion in benevolent intent. We are speaking about influence not for deceitful purposes, but for mutual gain and understanding. This chapter is chalked full of strategies and practices to help you become an ethical manipulator.

An ethical manipulator seeks to influence others by driving them towards beneficial decisions without violating their autonomy. It requires a deep understanding of human psychology, empathy, and effective communication.

*Human Psychology and Influence: An Introduction*

Understanding human psychology is the backbone of successful ethical manipulation. This knowledge allows you to tap into how people think, respond, and make decisions, enabling you to tailor your strategies to your audience effectively.

Human psychology primarily involves cognition (how we think), emotions (how we feel), and behavior (how we act). To influence effectively, you must appeal to these three entities seamlessly. Therefore, three cardinal rules of ethical manipulation surfacing from human psychology are simpler than expected: Understand your audience's thinking, appeal to their emotions, and influence their actions.

# 11.1. Understanding Your Audience

Getting under the skin of your audience and understanding their thought processes are instrumental in ethical manipulation. Begin by familiarizing yourself with their backgrounds, needs, aspirations, and fears - this intelligence facilitates connection, trust, and openness.

For businesses, this often involves creating customer personas or demographic profiles. Consult trusted literature, conduct surveys, and engage your audience in discussions to gather valuable information. For an everyday influence, you must be attentive and intuitive to people's verbal and non-verbal cues.

Once you possess this understanding, you are ready to tailor your persuasive approach accordingly.

## 11.2. Emotional Appeal

Emotion significantly influences human behavior. By evoking particular emotions, you can drive people to make specific decisions or take certain actions. Crucially, this must be done ethically and responsibly, without causing harm or distress.

When attempting to influence through emotions, understand the nature of emotions you want to evoke and the appropriate context. Positive emotions such as happiness, excitement, or nostalgia tend to open people up, making them more susceptible to influence - all while fostering a positive relationship.

## 11.3. Influencing Actions

Once you have appealed to your audience's thoughts and emotions, it's time to influence their actions. This stage involves employing specific tactics to encourage them to make decisions that align with your goal. Stick with us as we move onto some of the most effective strategies for achieving this.

These principles have been studied and validated in various contexts and situations, proving their effectiveness as strategies for ethical manipulation. Knowing these principles will not only boost your persuasion skills but will also make you more aware of others' attempts to influence you.

# 11.4. Reciprocity

This principle hinges on the human tendency to want to return a favor. Giving something of value — whether physical or intangible — can encourage others to give something back in return. In persuasive communication, this can range from offering helpful information to performing a kind gesture.

# 11.5. Social Proof

People often look to others for guidance, especially in uncertain situations. By demonstrating the acceptance or approval of others, you can persuade your audience to adopt a particular behavior, belief, or action.

# 11.6. Authority

People respect authority and are more likely to be influenced by individuals they perceive as authoritative or knowledgeable. Establishing your credibility or aligning yourself with an authority figure can enhance your persuasiveness.

# 11.7. Consistency and Commitment

People like to be consistent in their words and actions. If you can get someone to commit (verbally or in writing) to a small action or belief, they're more likely to commit to larger related requests later on.

## 11.8. Liking

People are more easily persuaded by people they like. Enhance your likability by building relationships, demonstrating empathy, or finding common ground with your audience.

## 11.9. Scarcity

The principle of scarcity states that people find items or opportunities more attractive if they're limited or hard to come by. You can use this principle ethically by highlighting unique benefits or exclusive opportunities.

No single strategy will work in all situations, and what is most effective will depend on the particular person and context. However, a deep understanding of these principles and a mindful application can considerably boost your influencing skills.

Take these principles as your arsenal in your journey to becoming an effective ethical manipulator. Deploy them as the situation requires, win people over, influence decisions with grace, and enjoy the thrill of evoking change for the greater good.

# Chapter 12. Mastering the Art of Storytelling: The Ultimate Persuasion Technique

In the grand theatre of human interactions, storytelling reigns supreme. From quaint anecdotes shared over dinner to grand stories recounted in global boardrooms, our craft of spinning narratives is an embodiment of our inherent need to connect, comprehend and, most importantly, persuade. Let's unravel its mystery together.

Stories, unlike dry facts and figures, stimulate our brains in ways that create deep, lasting connections. By harnessing the power of storytelling, we can engage our listeners and inspire them to action far more effectively than any other means of persuasion.

## 12.1. How Stories Drive Persuasion

When we think about persuasion, we often picture a glib salesperson touting their product, or a slick lawyer drilling down their case. However, persuasion is not merely confined to these scenarios. At its core, the persuasive power of storytelling resides in its ability to invoke empathy and emotions, create understanding, and foster a sense of shared experience.

But how exactly does a story accomplish this?

When you share a story, you aren't merely reciting a sequence of events. Instead, you are painting a vibrant picture that stimulates different areas of the brain. Neuroscientists have discovered that listening to narratives activates parts of the brain known to be involved in personal experiences and emotion processing, such as the posterior cingulate cortex, medial prefrontal cortex, and precuneus.

This neural activation engenders empathy in your listeners, triggering them to subconsciously mirror your feelings and perceptions. Such subconscious sharing of experiences fosters a deep psychic connection between you and your listener, strengthening your persuasive power.

## 12.2. Crafting a Compelling Story

Crafting a persuasive story might seem like a daunting task. However, like any art form, it's a skill that can be honed with the right understanding and practice. A successful persuasive narrative will generally comprise the following elements:

- A relatable protagonist: This gives your audience a character with whom to identify, promoting empathy.

- A conflict or challenge: This element adds intrigue and piques interest.

- A resolution: This offers a sense of closure and satisfaction.

- A moral or lesson: This binds the story together and underpins its persuasive intent.

Utilizing these elements in your storytelling creates a clear narrative structure that draws in your listener, evoking emotions and bonding them with the protagonist. This connection amplifies the persuasiveness of your story.

## 12.3. Inviting the Audience into the Narrative

While every story has a narrator, a truly persuasive story also has a co-creator – the audience. Inviting your audience into the narrative encourages them to participate actively in the story, rather than merely consuming it passively. This, in turn, enhances their engagement, creating a stronger emotional connection and elevating your persuasive power.

Interactive storytelling techniques could be as simple as using the second person narrative – "Imagine you are..." – to more sophisticated methods like rhetorical questions or creating opportunities for the audience to fill in the blanks.

Such strategies don't simply entertain or inform your audience – they enable them to see themselves in the story and feel part of its narrative arc. When your listeners become co-creators, they are more likely to internalize the story, draw personal relevance, and be persuaded in the process.

# 12.4. Harnessing Emotions in Storytelling

Evoking emotions is a corner-stone of persuasive storytelling. After all, humans are emotional beings, and our choices and decisions are greatly influenced by our feelings. By harnessing the power of emotions, we can motivate our listeners to take action.

Think about the stories that have moved you the most: They probably stirred up strong emotions within you, didn't they? The emotions evoked by storytelling stimulate the release of neurochemicals like oxytocin, popularly referred to as the "bonding hormone," which plays a significant role in social interaction and trust-building. By leveraging emotional narratives, you can connect viscerally with your audience and enhance your persuasiveness manifold.

# 12.5. The Ethical Aspects of Persuasive Storytelling

As with any form of persuasion, storytelling possesses remarkable power. Its capacity to influence and compel actions is immense. However, it's crucial to use this power responsibly, ethically, and considerately.

Remember, pursuing your persuasive goals should never necessitate manipulating your audience or distorting the truth. Instead, strive for authenticity and fairness in your storytelling. Honesty and integrity not only contribute to your credibility but strengthen your persuasive power by establishing trust with the audience.

In conclusion, storytelling, when done right, provides one of the most potent tools for persuasion. By incorporating empathy, engagement, emotional resonance, and ethical considerations into your storytelling strategy, you can elevate your persuasive prowess and influence others with ease. It's a craft as ancient as humanity itself – and an art we can all master with practice, understanding, and a bit of creative gusto. Let your stories ring true and speak loud, enchanting as they convince!

# Chapter 13. Harnessing Reciprocity: The Give-and-Take Influence

Our journey ventures first into one of the potent ways of persuasion: Harnessing Reciprocity - the alchemy of "give and take."

Reciprocity is an ingrained societal norm, a glue that creates, maintains, and strengthens human connections. It's our innate proclivity to repay what we receive. If someone does something nice for us, we naturally feel an impulse to do something nice in return.

## 13.1. Understanding Reciprocity

To begin understanding how reciprocity works, let's consider this scenario: you're fast rushing towards a closing elevator, and someone inside holds the door. By sharing a simple "Thank you", you've responded to the kind gesture. Next, you might chat about the weather, an act of reciprocating the initial spark of conversation. Here, reciprocity engages both parties in a cyclical pattern, visibly defining the "give and take" dynamics.

Speaking to the heart of human behaviour, reciprocity integrates into numerous sectors - from marketing strategies to etiquette norms, from leadership approaches to psychological treatments.

One famous experiment illuminating reciprocity was implemented by Dennis Regan in 1971. His subjects believed they were in a study about art appreciation. However, in the middle of this exercise, Regan's collaborator would exit and return with cokes. While some received a surprise coke (reciprocal condition), others didn't (control condition). Later, the collaborator asked participants to buy raffle tickets. Individuals who received the coke on average bought twice as many tickets, evidencing the power of reciprocity.

# 13.2. The Rule of Reciprocity

To employ reciprocity effectively, you need to grasp its three core elements: spontaneity, significance, and customization.

1. **Spontaneity:** The act should be unexpected. An unexpected gift fosters an immediate sense of indebtedness, thereby promoting a stronger urge to reciprocate.

2. **Significance:** The gift should be meaningful. The larger the gift in value (emotionally, not necessarily monetarily), the stronger the feeling of indebtedness.

3. **Customization:** The gift should feel personalized. A gift that's aligned with the receiver's needs, tastes, or interests produces greater reciprocity.

Each factor intensifies the urgency to repay, enhancing the influence you wield. However, employing this rule requires careful application, leveraging authenticity, and ethical considerations. Using reciprocity manipulatively can backfire, sour relationships, and tarnish reputations.

# 13.3. Reciprocity in Negotiations

In negotiations, reciprocity proves a vital strategy. Successful negotiators cleverly adopt the 'give-and-take' technique, where they willingly make concessions. However, these concessions aren't purely altruistic; they are made with the expectation of equivalent or greater concessions from the other party.

The success of such strategies lies in the negotiator's ability to demonstrate altruism convincingly. Here, the rule of proximity comes into play; the quicker the reciprocation occurs, the stronger the affinity between given and received favors.

## 13.4. Reciprocity in Marketing

Business and marketing realms are no strangers to the concept of reciprocity. Giving an unexpected 'gift' to potential or existing customers can improve relationships and induce return business. Free samples, bonus items, and complimentary services are all part of this practice.

Here, the 'give-and-take' is not immediate. The company 'gives', hoping that eventually, the customer will 'take' by making a purchase, subscribing, or promoting their products or services.

## 13.5. Guiding Principles

Here, we move to the guiding principles to elicit effective reciprocity.

1. **Give first and give unconditionally:** To catalyze the cycle of reciprocity, you must be the initiator. Avoid keeping score as it may create a transactional feeling, belying the principle of spontaneous and customized giving.

2. **Be consistent:** Build a reputation as a giver. Consistent giving helps you to formulate a positive, dependable image.

3. **Recognize the power of a small gesture:** Acts of kindness don't necessarily have to be grand. Often, it is the small gestures that leave a lasting impression.

4. **Reciprocate generously:** When you are at the receiving end, reciprocate generously. Gratitude fosters stronger connections, fostering a continuous cycle.

To conclude, mastering the art of reciprocity involves thoughtful application of its principles, keeping the approach genuine and ethically sound. Whether in personal relationships or professional settings, the power of reciprocity can bridge gaps, resolve conflicts, and establish lasting bonds. However, as with any other tool, the ethical application is crucial for mutual benefit and sustainable relationships. Always remember, the strength of reciprocity lies in its authenticity.

By harnessing the power of reciprocity, you hold a robust tool for persuasion, capable of positively influencing perspectives and behaviors while simultaneously nurturing relationships.

# Chapter 14. Authority: Its Power and How to Wield It Responsibly

An integral pillar of persuasion is Authority. It touches every sphere of our lives, from the courtroom to the classroom and even in our homes. Understanding the power of authority and learning how to wield it responsibly is undeniably significant if one hopes to use it as a tool for influence.

At the outset, it is important to understand what authority entails. Authority is derived from Latin 'auctoritas,' meaning invention, advice, opinion, influence, or command. It is traditionally defined as the power or right to give orders, make decisions, and enforce obedience. The impact that authority has on our behavior is undeniably strong, which is often why it is adopted as a principle of persuasion.

## 14.1. Anatomy of Authority

We are wired to respond to authority — it goes back to our primal instincts of survival. Obeying the alpha in a pack offered protection, food, and reproductive benefits to our ancestors. These traits passed down the generations and are ingrained within us. We naturally respond to figures of authority with compliance, respect, and even reverence.

In the field of psychology, multiple experiments demonstrate our unwavering obedience to authority, even when morally and ethically challenged — the most famous of which is the Milgram experiment. Participants were told to administer electric shocks to other participants, escalating in severity. Despite their discomfort and the apparent pain of the 'learner,' a substantial number obeyed the authoritative experimenter's instructions.

Understanding this response can help you in two ways. First, it provides a clue as to how one's assertions, suggestions, and commands can carry weight, affecting the behavior of others. Second, and perhaps more importantly, this knowledge offers an opportunity to be aware of how our own behavior and decision-making are influenced by perceived authority.

## 14.2. Asserting Your Authority

Asserting authority does not necessarily mean being a stern, commanding figure. It's much more nuanced than that. Authority is as much about perceived expertise, credibility, and leadership as it is about exerting power or control.

Your authority stems from your experience, knowledge, and skills. By showcasing your expertise, you can underscore your authority and thereby enhance your influence on others. Conversely, when establishing yourself as an authority figure, it is important to understand and fill the knowledge gaps, as these could undermine your credibility.

## 14.3. Using Authority Ethically: The Tangent of Responsibility

Despite its persuasive power, authority can become a destructive force if wielded irresponsibly. Unchecked authority can lead to domination, undermining of consent, or inciting harmful actions. This is an undue and unethical form of persuasion.

True and potent authority combines the understanding of its influence with the wisdom of its measured use. Deploying your authority should adhere to the principle of minimal force — using the least amount of pressure or influence to evoke the desired action or result.

Responsibility also translates into authenticity. Your authority is not just about your knowledge and skills; it's about your ability to connect with people on a human level. This aligns with Aristotle's concept of Ethos, appealing to credibility or character.

# Chapter 15. Building Authority: A Step-by-Step Approach

Even the most knowledgeable individuals can struggle to assert authority effectively. This section provides some practical steps to build and assert your authority, helping to foster a position of influence:

1. Demonstrate Expertise: Your knowledge in your domain is the foundation of your authority. Encourage others to recognize this. Share your thoughts, offer insights, and provide solutions that reflect your depth of understanding.

2. Show Consistency: Consistency fosters trust, thereby reinforcing your authority. Be reliable in your actions, decisions, and advice.

3. Speak with Confidence: Confidence in yourself reinforces others' faith in your authority. A well-delivered message can be very impactful.

4. Embrace Empathy: Understand the perspectives of others. This shows your respect for their viewpoints, reinforcing your authority and their willingness to accept it.

5. Engage in Active Listening: Authority comes with the responsibility to listen and understand the needs and concerns of your audience.

# 15.1. Conclusion: Authority and the Power of Influence

The power of authority, when combined with the fundamental principles of influence, can create powerful persuasive synergies.

Done effectively and ethically, authority can not only drive compliance but also inspire and motivate others toward shared goals.

Remember, authority is not about controlling or overpowering. It's about leading, guiding, teaching, and, most importantly, inspiring. Wield it responsibly for it can shape actions, mold opinions, and steer outcomes profoundly.

For a deeper dive into associated topics and hands-on exercises to apply your newly acquired knowledge, stay tuned for the next sections in this Special Report.

# Chapter 16. Consistency and Commitment: Building Trust to Influence Effectively

It all begins with building a relationship based on trust. Trust is the foundation of any meaningful relationship. Whether it involves intimate partners, friendships, business relationships, or even the nuanced relationship between a speaker and audience, a web of trust is inevitably woven. And this trust is not built overnight; it requires consistency and commitment from all parties involved.

## 16.1. The Psychology of Consistency

Psychologists affirm that human beings are creatures of habit.

We feel comfortable if we're surrounded by familiarity and consistency. They allow us to establish a sense of control, to predict outcomes, and to manage our lives effectively. Therefore, we tend to surround ourselves with events, relationships, and even ideologies that maintain a significant level of consistency with our existing belief systems and behaviors.

This notion has been leveraged as a powerful tool in the world of persuasion. A consistent person is often viewed as reliable, trustworthy, and rational, which are highly desirable qualities in both personal and professional relationships. Therefore, by demonstrating consistency, particularly in our words and actions, we can pave the way for becoming more influential.

So, how does one embed the principle of consistency into their persuasive techniques?

First, it starts with self-consistency. This means being consistent with your own beliefs, values, and actions. If you walk your talk, people are more likely to respect and trust you. Disparities between your rhetoric and behavior will only create an impression of dishonesty or unreliability.

Second, encourage consistency in others. When people publicly commit to something, they are more likely to follow through simply to appear consistent in the eyes of others. So, when trying to persuade someone, guide them to commit openly to their actions.

# 16.2. The Importance of Commitment in Building Trust

Commitment fundamentally complements consistency.

In a relationship context, commitment conveys a promise of investment, time, and undivided loyalty. In a persuasion scenario, it influences perceived reliability, credibility, and accountability, essentially becoming the backbone of trust.

Evidently, a deep commitment to the persuader's cause often translates into a heightened influence over the listener. The mere act of expressing commitment may even evoke a reciprocal promise, thereby fabricating a mutual trust that helps further the persuader's cause.

Public declarations are a remarkable way to establish commitment. Encouraging someone to make a public commitment can significantly increase their obligation towards a cause or an idea.

Surely, you must consider the ethics of commitment. It's crucial to induce commitments genuinely and ethically. Attempts to manipulate or pressure someone into a commitment will ultimately damage trust and credibility.

## 16.3. The Role of Consistency and Commitment in Persuasion

So, how do consistency and commitment typically come into play in a real-world context?

There are numerous techniques and strategies designed around these two principles. Some common strategies include the 'foot-in-the-door' technique, and the 'low-ball' technique.

The 'foot-in-the-door' technique involves getting someone to agree to a small request first, thereby committing them to the cause or principle. Owing to the instinct to be consistent, once they agree to the smaller task, they are more likely to agree to larger, related requests.

The 'low-ball' technique operates similarly. Initially, a simple, attractive deal is offered. Once the person agrees, they typically feel committed to the transaction, even if the terms are altered slightly to their disadvantage.

Remember, these strategies should always be deployed ethically. Using them manipulatively could quickly demolish your credibility.

## 16.4. Embracing the Power of Consistency and Commitment

The beauty of these principles lies in their applicability to various aspects of life.

Whether in marketing a product, promoting a social cause, negotiating a business deal, or spurring community-level change, the psychological power of consistency and commitment can be harnessed to enhance influence and drive durable change in attitudes and behaviors.

To recap, consistency establishes your credibility, and commitment strengthens the bond of trust between you and your audience. Together, they build a solid foundation that paves the route to effective persuasion. However, using them requires an ethical approach consistent with your values to avoid losing credibility.

In conclusion, embrace consistency and commitment as the key principles in your playbook. And remember, what truly matters is not just the power to persuade, but the ability to do so responsibly and ethically. Build trust, show your dedication, and let your authenticity blossom. In the grand theater of persuasion, these virtues are your magic keys to influence!

# Chapter 17. Charm with Charisma: The Irresistible Allure of Personal Magnetism

Charisma: some people seem to be born with it, shimmering and sparkling, while for others, it remains a coveted trait lurking just out of reach. But the truth is, charisma is not just an innate quality. Rather, it's a potent blend of certain skills and behaviors that anyone can learn and cultivate with a little bit of practice and perseverance. The power of charisma, when combined with the art and science of persuasion, broadens horizons, cracks open doors of opportunities, and lights up pathways to accomplishment.

Dive into the world of charismatic allure, identify the components of charisma, and apply the lessons in this chapter to become an irresistible, influential figure in your own right.

## 17.1. The Anatomy of Charisma

Charisma is often regarded as a mystical, intangible trait. In reality, it is a concoction of a few simple, yet crucial, elements: presence, power, and warmth.

Presence refers to being in the moment, paying full attention to the other person, and responding to them authentically. Power, in the context of charisma, is not about domination but the demonstration of competence and confidence. Warmth has to do with displaying goodwill and kindheartedness towards others.

Let's dissect these elements further.

1. Presence: Being Fully There Presence reflects the degree to which you're fully engaged in the present moment, rather than

preoccupied with past errors or future anxieties. This involves active listening, consistent eye contact, and acknowledging what the other person says.

2. Power: Knowing and Showing Your Worth Power is about showing your confidence and competence. This doesn't mean bragging about your accomplishments blatantly, rather, it's about the subtle demonstration of your competence. Using affirmative language, maintaining an upright posture, and demonstrating emotional stability are all attributes of this power.

3. Warmth: Forging Deep Connections Warmth is perceived as the probability that you will use whatever power you have in favor of others. It involves empathy, benevolence, and a genuine interest in others' wellbeing. Positive body language, friendly tone, and willingness to help are key indicators of warmth.

By cultivating these three core elements, you can become a charismatic person that easily wins the hearts and minds of the people around you.

# 17.2. The Role of Emotional Intelligence

Emotional intelligence (EQ) plays a pivotal role in charismatic appeal. A high EQ demonstrates adaptability to varying social situations and aids in making deep, meaningful connections. The dimensions of emotional intelligence – self-awareness, self-regulation, social skills, empathy, and motivation – are all closely interwoven with the aspects of charisma.

1. Self-Awareness: Understanding ourselves, knowing our strengths, weaknesses, emotions, and drives is the first step towards developing charisma.

2. Self-Regulation: Ability to control or redirect disruptive impulses and moods, and the propensity to suspend judgment and think

before acting.

3. Social Skills: Proficiency in managing relationships, building networks, and understanding the emotional currents in negotiation and solution discussions aid in persuasive communication.

4. Empathy: To be charismatic, understanding other's emotional make-up, treating people according to their emotional reactions is crucial.

5. Motivation: Having a passion to work for reasons that go beyond money and status.

Remember, emotional intelligence can be improved over time. So can charisma. Both go hand in hand in building meaningful connections.

# 17.3. Building Personal Charm through Effective Communication

Effective communication is vital in making a charismatic impact. Charm doesn't exist in a vacuum; it's built and sustained through our interactions with others. Here's how to utilize effective communication:

1. Tailoring Your Message: Know your audience and their needs. Modify your language, tone, and illustrations to suit their understanding and relatability.

2. Non-Verbal Signals: Use positive and open body language. Maintain eye contact, use natural gestures, and orient your body towards the person you're communicating with.

3. Active Listening: Show genuine interest while listening to others. Reflect understanding by nodding and using positive affirmations.

4. Positive Affirmations: Use positive and encouraging words. This

encourages the other person to express more comfortably.

# 17.4. The Ethics of Charm: Using Charisma for Good

While charisma can be a potent tool for persuasion, it's essential to use it ethically. Charm shouldn't be a mechanism of manipulation but a means to foster healthy and authentic connections. Balance your charisma with sincerity and empathy and use your persuasive power for the greater good.

Absolutely anyone can be charismatic, given some practice and perseverance. Like any skill, it requires active cultivation and maintenance. Once you've mastered it, your abilities to influence, inspire, and bond will expand immeasurably. So go forth and radiate that irresistible allure you've now unlocked!